Whitney's Birthday Party

Written by
Madeline Tyler

Illustrated by
Ryo Arata

Whitney was spoilt. Wherever she was and whatever she was doing, it was always: "I want this, I want that!"

Whitney's Birthday Party

PHASE 5

7a

Level 7 – Turquoise

BookLife

Helpful Hints for Reading at Home

The graphemes (written letters) and phonemes (units of sound) used throughout this series are aligned with Letters and Sounds. This offers a consistent approach to learning whether reading at home or in the classroom. Books levelled as 'a' are an introduction to this band. Readers can advance to 'b' where graphemes are consolidated and further graphemes are introduced.

HERE IS A LIST OF ALTERNATIVE GRAPHEMES FOR THIS PHASE OF LEARNING. AN EXAMPLE OF THE PRONUNCIATION CAN BE FOUND IN BRACKETS.

Phase 5 Alternative Pronunciations of Graphemes			
a (hat, what)	e (bed, she)	i (fin, find)	o (hot, so)
u (but, unit)	c (cat, cent)	g (got, giant)	ow (cow, blow)
ie (tied, field)	ea (eat, bread)	er (farmer, herb)	ch (chin, school, chef)
y (yes, by, very)	ou (out, shoulder, could, you)		
o_e (home)	u_e (rule)		

HERE ARE SOME WORDS WHICH YOUR CHILD MAY FIND TRICKY.

Phase 5 Tricky Words			
oh	their	people	Mr
Mrs	looked	called	asked
could			

HERE ARE SOME WORDS THAT MIGHT NOT YET BE FULLY DECODABLE.

Challenge Words			
party	couldn't	ready	hungry

TOP TIPS FOR HELPING YOUR CHILD TO READ:

• Allow children time to break down unfamiliar words into units of sound and then encourage children to string these sounds together to create the word.

• Encourage your child to point out any focus phonics when they are used.

• Read through the book more than once to grow confidence.

• Ask simple questions about the text to assess understanding.

• Encourage children to use illustrations as prompts.

PHASE 5

7a

This book is an 'a' level and is a turquoise level 7 book band.

Whitney wanted Murph to help her plan her birthday party. But Murph was sick of Whitney always whinging whenever she didn't get her way.

"What about a dressing up party in the garden?" said Murph.
"No, no, no!" whinged Whitney. "I want a party at Banana Forest!"

"But a party at Banana Forest costs too much money," said Murph. "A dressing up party will be fun! Whoever has the best outfit can win a prize!"

Whitney didn't want to dress up, but she did want to win the prize. "Maybe a dressing up party is a good idea," she whispered.

"Phew," said Murph. "Now, who do you want to invite to your party?"
"No one! I want the prize all to myself!" said Whitney.

"But what about all of your friends?" asked Murph. "There's Ralph the whale, Sal the mouse, Whiskers the cat and Blue the dolphin!"

"Maybe playing with my friends is better than winning the prize," said Whitney.
"I will phone all your friends and tell them about the party!" said Murph.

"What a good idea!" they all cheered. "We love dressing up!"
"Me too!" whispered Sal the mouse into the telephone.

Next, Murph and Whitney needed to plan what to have at the party. "Where shall we start?" asked Murph.
"The food!" said Whitney.

Whitney wanted banana cake, banana sweets and banana pie. She wanted the whole garden to be filled with bananas!

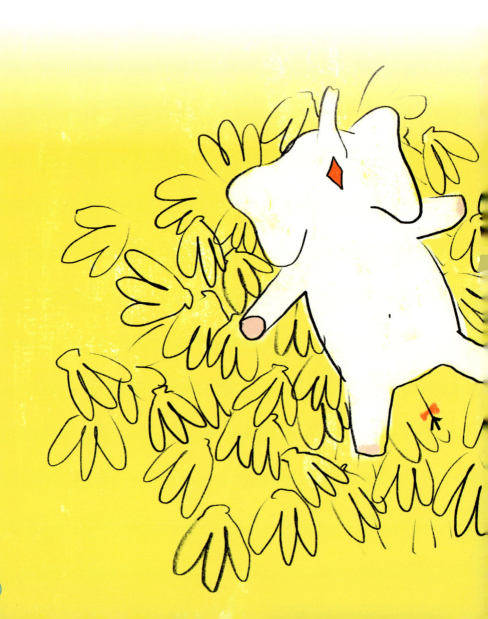

Bananas were Whitney's best food.
She had them for lunch, for dinner and as
a snack. She had bananas whenever she got
her trunk on them!

"We need to have different sorts of food for all your friends," said Murph.
"Why? All animals love bananas!" replied Whitney, munching on a banana.

"Not all animals love bananas," said Murph. "Whiskers loves fish, and Sal's best food is cheese! What about if we have a mixture of foods?"

Whitney was upset. It was her birthday party and she wanted there to be bananas! So, she whinged, and whinged, and whinged...

Whitney didn't stop whinging until Murph showed her all the party food. She had a whiff. It smelled good, even if it wasn't all bananas.

The food was all set, but what next?
"Balloons!" said Murph and Whitney.
"I want balloons that look like bananas!"
said Whitney.

"But Blue likes flower balloons, and Ralph's favourite balloons are always pink," said Murph. "Why don't we have lots of different balloons?"

Maybe Whitney couldn't always get what she wanted, even on her birthday. Whitney still wanted banana treats and banana balloons, but she wanted something else even more.

Whitney wanted all her friends to have fun at her party. She just needed to get her outfit ready before they all arrived...

There was a knock on the door. Whitney's friends had arrived for the party, but they were too soon! Whitney was not ready yet!

"Oh no!" said Whitney. "I have not dressed up! What will I do? I will never win the prize now!" But then the door opened and...

They were all dressed up just like Whitney. They were all elephants! There was Sal the elephant and Whiskers the elephant...

HAPPY WHITNE

And even Ralph and Blue the elephants!
"Surprise!" said all her friends. "Can you tell
who we are?"
Whitney was not dressed up, but it didn't
matter after all.

Whitney had a photo taken with all her elephant friends. "I think you need to have the prize, Murph. Thank you for the best party ever!"

"Why don't we all have it?" said Murph. Whitney tucked into banana pie, Sal nibbled on some cheese, and they all had the best day ever.

Whitney's Birthday Party

1. What did Whitney want Murph to help her plan?

2. What food does Whitney love most of all?

    (a) Bananas

    (b) Grapes

    (c) Oranges

3. Why do you think Whitney kept whinging?

4. What costumes were Whitney's friends wearing?

5. Do you think Murph deserved to win the prize? What would you have said to Whitney if you were helping to plan her party?

©2020 **BookLife Publishing Ltd.**
King's Lynn, Norfolk PE30 4LS

ISBN 978–1–83927–306–3

Whitney's Birthday Party
Written by Madeline Tyler
Illustrated by Ryo Arata

An Introduction to BookLife Readers...

Our Readers have been specifically created in line with the London Institute of Education's approach to book banding and are phonetically decodable and ordered to support each phase of the Letters and Sounds document.

Each book has been created to provide the best possible reading and learning experience. Our aim is to share our love of books with children, providing both emerging readers and prolific page–turners with beautiful books that are guaranteed to provoke interest and learning, regardless of ability.

BOOK BAND GRADED using the Institute of Education's approach to levelling.

PHONETICALLY DECODABLE supporting each phase of Letters and Sounds.

EXERCISES AND QUESTIONS to offer reinforcement and to ascertain comprehension.

BEAUTIFULLY ILLUSTRATED to inspire and provoke engagement, providing a variety of styles for the reader to enjoy whilst reading through the series.

AUTHOR INSIGHT:
MADELINE TYLER

Native to Norfolk, England, Madeline Tyler's intelligence and professionalism can be felt in the 50–plus books that she has written for BookLife Publishing. A graduate of Queen Mary University of London with a 1st Class degree in Comparative Literature, she also received a University Volunteering Award for helping children to read at a local school.

When she was a child, Madeline enjoyed playing the violin, and she now relaxes through yoga and reading books!

PHASE 5

7a

This book is an 'a' level and is a turquoise level 7 book band.